To my d[...]
Lorriane.
on the bi[...]
new Grandchildren.
Thankyou for introducing
me to God + JeFF Lucas!
                          x
Much love to you +
Grandpa Roy! + the girls.
             x
    Rachael xx
              x

THINGS MY GRANDCHILDREN TAUGHT ME

Copyright © Jeff Lucas, 2012

Published by CWR, Waverley Abbey House,
Waverley Lane, Farnham, Surrey GU9 8EP, England.

CWR is a Registered Charity – Number 294387
and a Limited Company registered in England –
Registration Number 1990308.

The right of Jeff Lucas to be identified as the author of this work has been asserted
by him in accordance with the Copyright, Designs and Patents Act 1988.

For a list of National Distributors, visit www.cwr.org.uk/distributors

Concept development, editing, design and production by CWR

Cover image: Melanie Ray

Photographs: Ben Wilkes p.7, Melanie Ray pp.14,54;
Jeff Lucas p.16; istockphoto p.61; Fotosearch (all other pages)

Printed in Slovenia by Florjancic Tisk

ISBN: 978-1-85345-922-1

THINGS MY GRANDCHILDREN TAUGHT ME

Jeff Lucas

CWR

Dedicated to the grandfather

that Stanley and Alexander have yet to meet:

David Thomas Wilkes, (1947-2008)

From one grandparent to another …

Being a grandparent. There's nothing quite like it.

It's a club that most are thrilled to join. For some, it's payback for hair that's grey, or vanishing. For all, it's compensation for ageing.

It's a grand title, literally.

Grandparent.

Being a grandparent is one of the greatest experiences on earth. It's so good, we love to share it.

Some grandparents are so excited, they're dangerous.
An enthusiastic grandparent can seriously disrupt your day.

Armed to the teeth with photos, given the chance, they'll whip them out of their wallets like a quick-on-the-draw gunfighter. Tech-savvy grandparents with smartphones are even more adept. They're eager to share all 3,000 snaps of their darlings. Sit down for an hour or three, why don't you …?

And grandparents chatter on about their grandchildren breathlessly, and endlessly, offering fascinating updates to anyone who will listen. Actually, they'll talk to anyone who is too timid to flee.

'Great news! Our little Suzy burped for the first time yesterday, it was absolutely marvellous.
She's so clever, you know ...'

'James smeared strawberry jam all over the new television ...
he's very creative. We think he's going to be a surrealist artist ...'

And when we grandparents bump into each other, we loudly celebrate our lot in life, for we are most blessedly ... grandparents.

Delighted to meet fellow members of the club, we exchange well-worn clichés, pretending we're hearing them for the first time.

'It's great, isn't it? You get to spoil them
and then give them back ...'

'Being a grandparent is so good, I wish I could have skipped parenting and just gone straight to the grandparental part ...'

I have two grandchildren, Stanley and Alexander. They've stolen my heart. One of their broad smiles can transform my day. I confess, I'm besotted. And watching them, listening to them, has taught me so much, hence this book.

If you're a grandparent, soak up the gravy of every moment: it's not forever. And if you're not, bribe your children, and encourage them to produce, promptly.

I'll say it again.

Being a grandparent. There's nothing quite like it.

It's possible to assume a facial expression of concentration that suggests that you are pondering the meaning of life, and are therefore quite the genius, when in fact you are just filling another nappy.

NOT EVERYONE WHO LOOKS CLEVER, IS.

Alex's brow is furrowed, ploughed by the intensity of the moment. The jaw is set, determined. And the eyes are clamped tight, shutting out all distraction. Hush, please. One is surely in the presence of greatness.

Brilliance needs space.

Perhaps a new breakthrough is at hand, or a previously unfathomable mathematical conundrum is about to be solved. Wisdom is fermenting.

But perhaps there's a more mundane reason for all that grimacing. Your grandchild is not exercising the mind, but the bowels.

There's no delicate way to put this.

They're not pondering anything.

They're pooing.

Some people just naturally look like they're brighter, wiser, wittier and quicker than the rest of us. And some are accomplished at the dubious art of just *looking* clever, regardless of whether they are or not. They have a practised air of superiority, wearing a poker-faced look of disdain on their faces, tut-tutting and rolling their eyes at lesser mortals. They snigger, and sometimes even sneer. But their expressions don't guarantee their intelligence.

They're just good at arranging their facial muscles. We need to remember that, next time that wet blanket feeling of inferiority is suddenly draped across our shoulders.

Surely you know that sinking feeling.

You're desperately making small talk at a party, a conversation dwindles to an end, and you scan the room, trying to locate another victim to discuss the weather with. You take in the hum of bright, intelligent sounding chatter, and you suddenly feel ... less.

Suddenly everyone else seems more clever, more attractive and more interesting than you.

And you're probably quite wrong.
Don't judge a book by its cover, however impressive, or unimpressive, it might be. And don't assume that because someone looks clever it means that they are.

Don't live intimidated.

Fashion is *your* choice, not the decision of some designer who lives in Milan. If you think it looks good, that's good enough.

Stanley wears whatever he chooses, within reason.
One day he sports a flat cap like a junior Yorkshireman.
And then suddenly he's all dressed up for a treasure
hunt, because he's a feisty buccaneer, complete with
eye patch and plastic sword. Or a fireman – his current
favourite fashion choice. His fluorescent yellow
helmet means you could spot him from Pluto.

Grandparents will remember the era of the seventies, surely a season of fashion insanity. We staggered around on platform heels, the air definitely thinner up there. Chaps wore jackets with lapels so wide, a strong wind could have swept them to Sydney. We sweated in horrid pseudo-fabrics like bri-nylon and Crimplene®. What possessed us to drape our bodies in such truly horrendous styles?

fashion

be you

It's simple.

We're creatures of the herd.

We slip easily into uniforms.

Someone, somewhere informed us that
this was the way to look cool, and we,
lemming-like, believed, obeyed, and
spent a decade looking ridiculous.

So go ahead, buy a stuffed parrot to adorn your
shoulder if you like, and be you. And not the
version of you that someone else says you must be.

You can be in a screaming tantrum at noon and giggling with laughter at 12.02pm. Your current mood doesn't have to last all day. Or all year.

mood

Some of us decide our mood the moment
our eyes flicker open in the morning.
We set ourselves on emotional cruise
control, insisting that we got out of bed
the wrong side, which we probably did
not. We frown and mutter and sulk
our way through the dreary hours that
follow, filing another irreplaceable part
of our lives under the heading of
'one of those days'.

And I've met a few eternally miserable
souls who apparently chose their mood
for life at birth. Perhaps they got upset
with the midwife for that light tap on
the bottom: don't you slap me ...

I'm not talking about depression,
which is a serious illness. I'm talking
moodiness. Self-absorbed irritability.
Becoming a prickly person, surrounded by
eggshells. Everyone who knows us tiptoes
around, fearful of walking on them.

But grandchildren teach us that
we can be in tears one moment,
and laughing out loud the next.

Moods aren't set in stone. We can choose
a smile over a growl, replace whining with
gratitude, and be pleasant rather than tetchy.

And if someone insists on staying grouchy,
just blow a huge raspberry on their belly.
A giggle will soon follow. This could be a
useful tactic in international diplomacy.

Or maybe not.

Keep growing.

Passing wind at the meal

table is adorable at 18 months.

Don't try it when you're 54.

Grandchildren win applause for the most unusual achievements. A table side 'toot', as it's politely tagged, especially one accompanied by a squeal of delight, is likely to be greeted by hearty congratulations from adoring relatives. Even naughtiness, when your grandchild decorates daddy's head with dinner, can win thinly disguised approval.

But there won't be any standing ovations if you try either of these stunts as an adult. Tooting food-fighters aren't popular guests at dinner parties.

Everything changes. And so should we.

Let's keep growing,
and never bow to the belief that
we're sentenced to sameness.
We can be different.

Today.

It doesn't matter what the moves look like. If you call it dancing, then it's dancing.

We were in a t-shirt shop, a colourful place reverberating with loud, summery music. Suddenly Stanley launched into some moves. His dancing was chaotic and uncoordinated. An uplifted arm here, a kick of the leg there, a dizzy twirl and a jerk of the head. Soon others were joining in, clapping and hopping from one foot to the other. Grandma doesn't normally dance in shops. She did that day.

Dancing.

It's not supposed to be strict, or 'strictly', but it's about moving to music. Go ahead, mix it up, have fun, break step. We fret endlessly about what others think of us, which is odd. Most of them are strangers, so we'll never see them again.

Generally we'll never find out what they think. And frankly, it doesn't really matter anyway. Don't be a slave to other people's opinions.

have *fun*

Every time you see a plane
passing overhead, point up at it
and look amazed.
DON'T EVER GRADUATE
FROM BEING SURPRISED.

Grandchildren are good
at gawping amazement.
Mouth-wide-open wonder.

A distant jet, miles up in a blue sky.

The absurdly horned rhino in the safari
park. The twinge of a fishing rod that
says that dinner is on the line.

A fluorescent sunset.
The hop-skip-and-jump of a lamb.

Grandchildren are newcomers to the planet,
and spend a lot of their time being stunned
as they settle into their surroundings.

But for most of us, wonder is a
casualty, left behind us as we grew up.

Remember that eyes-like-saucers
amazement that was your companion
when you were a child?

You asked a million questions.

Relished new discoveries.

You were often shocked.

But then you settled down into been-there, done-that boredom. Perhaps you decided that you'd gathered enough information to get by, and now you're bored with life, on track to being bored to death.

Live with your eyes wide open again.
Book an appointment with a sunset.
Sign up for a course. Crack open a Russian novel.
Paddle in a rock pool. Learn a new language.

eyes
wide open

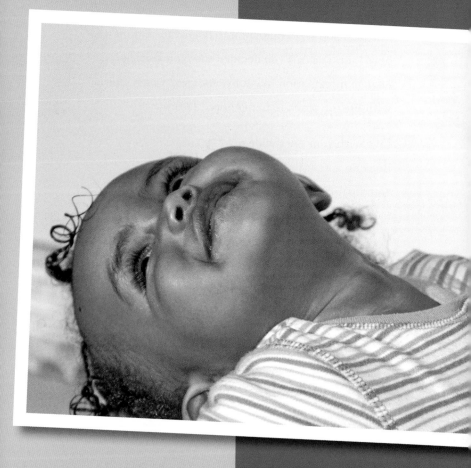

wonder

Life can be tough, bewildering,
and at times, devastating.

But there's always wonder,
if we know where to look.

When your Uncle Buck is 6,000 miles away, pick up his photograph and plant two kisses on it. When he hears what you did, the kisses will land on his faraway face. Love says so.

Being loved shouldn't involve guesswork:
we should know for sure. Uncle Buck
(his real name is Richard) lives in the
USA, so Stanley doesn't see him often.
Hence the kiss on the picture frame.
He was delighted when he heard about
that spontaneous peck on the cheek.

*If you love someone,
tell them. Creatively.*

But most of all, frequently.

tell them

Assume everyone, everywhere loves or likes you, until they prove you wrong.

Many of us spend our lives shadow boxing.

We live anxiously, hoping that we'll be approved of. And that means we can live neurotically. We see a quizzical look, we hear a certain tone of voice, and we assume: they don't like me.

Most grandchildren don't engage in that self-torment.

Stanley and Alex assume that the whole world loves them. Of course, that's not true, and unguarded trust could make them vulnerable. But I'd love some of their idealism about being loved. When you walk into a room, why not assume everyone loves you, until they prove otherwise? That way, you won't ruin the day by shadow boxing. It's an exhausting sport.

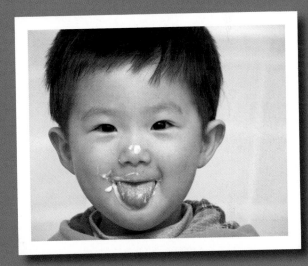

Your grandchild might be just like you. This is glorious, and terrifying.

*Look at our grandchildren,
and we're looking at a
part of us.*

If we had never been, then neither
would they – which is wonderful, and
mildly troubling, because they may have
inherited some of our weaknesses. Like
my never-ending 'lostness', for example.

part of us

I'm always lost when driving. I do stop and ask for directions, but quickly get bored while listening. Despite an in-built GPS system and a rather posh map, we often experience navigational tension in our car.

Stanley turned breech the day before he was born; gentlemen, that means he was facing the wrong way. 'I'm worried that he might have inherited his grandfather's sense of direction', smiled Ben, our son in law. 'There was only one exit, and he missed it.'

Yikes.

We often make life more
complicated than it needs to be.

It's a little routine that I dread
when we go for a drive:
fastening Stanley into his child's seat.

Those safety seats are designed by people who want
to protect children from accidents, and exasperate
the grandparents who have to buckle them in.

It ought to be a simple, twenty-second
procedure. Clunk, click, let's take a trip.

simple

Instead, it's an exacting test. Embarrassed, you fumble for the three straps that are supposed to easily clip together. Lining up metal clasp with metal clasp, you fiddle and huff and puff and try this way and that ...

The process isn't helped by the squirming of the three-year-old who is (a) not wanting to sit in the car seat in the first place (b) trying to fasten the straps himself and thus make his grandparent appear like a bumbling fool or worse still (c) sitting quietly with a condescending facial expression that says, 'Wow, how did you ever make it this far through life, and yet you can't fasten just three straps without all this sweating and muttering?'

So I had been struggling with the straps for about ten minutes when Stanley looked at me and murmured, 'It's not a puzzle, Granddad'.

Note to self: read the instructions. Then life would be less puzzling.

There are some phrases that we never really stop saying, or feeling. One of them is, 'look at me'.

Stanley enjoys wobbling along the High Street on his scooter, which he treats like a skateboard. He likes me to act as a mule, pulling him along. Today, he blurted out 'Look at my skills, Granddad'.

We're all born with a need — for an audience. Children want us to see them as they kick the ball, scuttle down the slide, or perform in one of their makeshift plays.

look

att

We want to be noticed, because we're
human, and not because we're show-offs.

Give people your full attention,
and you give them a priceless gift.
Listen. Ask questions.
Be genuinely interested.

Look.

Life demands a story.

'Tell me a story, Granddad ...'

I reach for a book, but Stanley shakes his
head. 'No, Granddad, make one up.'

I love this, because the stories don't have to follow
any logical sequence. I can chronicle a day in
the life of an octopus called Sid, who works at
a bank and whose best friend is a polka-dotted
gerbil. No matter that my tale is absurd.

Stanley absolutely relishes stories.

Stories are more than a prelude to bedtime.

Stories don't just entertain.

Stories teach us values, possibilities, and
build the muscle of the imagination.

Deprive a child of stories and we leave them nervous, unscripted, unable to make sense of the unfolding drama of which they are a part, the one called life.

Open that book, or make a story up. But know that stories are the foundation stones of life.

How much you enjoy something
is not necessarily related to
the price you paid for it.

You select the toy with meticulous care. Are the colours right? Does it look sufficiently interesting? Will it break at first play? At last, you make your choice, and hand over your credit card, which, because of the price of toys these days, takes a serious dent.

Alex is delighted, and gets hours of entertainment — by playing with the box, which, apparently, is more interesting than its pricey contents. The toy (£50) is ignored, and the box it came in (20p) is fascinating.

Some of the best things in life aren't
costly. And because something is pricey
it doesn't increase its potential to please.

Prayer is about saying
whatever's on your mind.

say what you think

Just down the lane where we live, there's
a beautiful eleventh-century church with
tumble-down gravestones and rich oak pews.

We often pause there during our family
strolls. We peer inside at the stained
glass tinged light of the church, and then
we take our places for the 'service'.

Stanley likes to climb into the pulpit, and
'preach'. This begins with him saying a
prayer. It's rambling, and beautiful with it.

'Dear Lord, thank You for loving us all. May all the daddies and mummies know about it, and may Pirate Pete and Fireman Sam get to put the fire out, and I'm going to play on my climbing frame, and the slide, and the trampoline, and I'd like an ice cream with chocolate on it ... and make Helen better. Amen.'

God is not looking for speeches, oratory, or a string of carefully crafted clever sentences.

Prayer can be a question put, a tear shed, a rant yelled, a thanks murmured.

Say what you think to God, and not what you think you're supposed to say.

The future. The past.

What are they?

NOW IS ALL THAT THERE IS.

Grandchildren are gifted at being fully present in the moment. They look forward to treats to come, but don't postpone their joy because of them.

Some of us live on *Someday Isle*, the land of anticipation. When we're older, fitter, thinner, on holiday, in a different home – then someday we'll be happy. Someday. We spend our whole lives indefinitely preparing to live.

And then, we relocate to a land much beloved by grandparents. It's called *Memory Lane*. We live in the past, not realising that the best of what was wasn't quite as great as we remember. And even if it was, to be blunt, it no longer exists.

While I'm being blunt, let's face this mildly unpalatable thought: perhaps the best of what is to come won't be as good as we hope.

Daydreaming means that we're sleeping through this moment, squandering it, choosing nostalgia or anticipation over what is actually happening now.

Live in this minute. Be fully present, especially when those grandchildren are around. The television can wait. The lawn can be mowed later.

But those grandchildren are growing up fast.